Chesters Roman
and the Clayton Museum

Nick Hodgson

CONTENTS

Tour of the Site

SETTING AND FORT LAYOUT

Chesters overlooks the river North Tyne, immediately to its east. The fort faces north and is playing-card shaped with a main gate in each side (see plan on the inside back cover). The fort covers an area of 2.33ha (5.75 acres). The stone fort wall, some 1.5m (5ft) wide, backed by a rampart of earth, is only visible at a few points where it has been excavated. Similarly there is little to see of the multiple ditches that surrounded the fort, as these have been levelled.

Descending from the hillside to the east, Hadrian's Wall was carried across the river by an impressive bridge. Substantial remains from this bridge can still be seen on the eastern bank of the river. The Wall runs up from the bridge to join the side of the fort just south of the east gate, and it resumes, leaving the fort, on the south side of the west gate. Originally it ran all the way through, the addition of the fort being a change of plan. Almost half the fort, and three of its gates, project north of the Wall.

From the west gate the Wall runs through trees to pass under Chesters house on its course westwards. Since the usual main side gates were isolated on the north side of the Wall, two extra gates (*portae quintanae*) gave access to the fort on the south side of the Wall and were entered by the Military Way, the Roman road running along the rear (south) of the Wall. These minor gates had a single passage and are a design feature only found in the forts on Hadrian's Wall.

Above: The head from a small ceramic figurine, possibly of the Emperor Augustus, found at Chesters
Below: Plan of Chesters Roman Fort, begun in about AD 124, showing its relation to the Military Way, Vallum and Wall, and the surrounding milecastles and turrets

Facing page: View of the baths at Chesters from across the North Tyne. Remains of the eastern abutment of the Roman bridge can be seen in the foreground

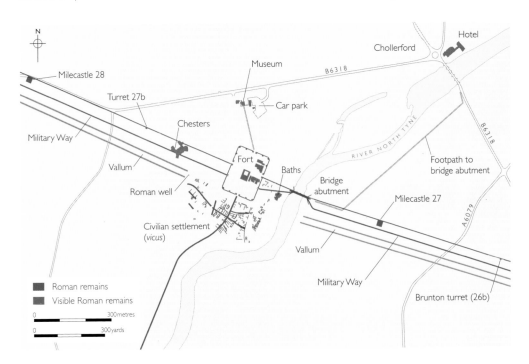

Above: The north gate with its
eastern tower in the foreground.
This was the ceremonial front gate
(porta praetoria) of the fort, though
little used by everyday traffic
Below: Weapons found at Chesters
A Spearhead
B Arrowheads
C Caltrops, designed to be thrown
   in the path of horses to impede
   enemy cavalry

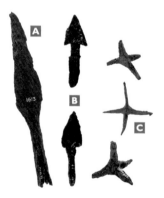

∎ NORTH GATE

The path approaching the fort from the site entrance heads
for a prominent grass-covered bank, marking the northern
rampart. The visitor arrives at the north gate, which in the
Roman period would only have been used to gain access to
the area north of Hadrian's Wall; the everyday entrances for
travellers along the Wall were the minor east and west gates,
while the south gate was used by those arriving via the civilian
settlement (vicus) to the south of the fort.

The north gate was one of four identical main gates and
the basic elements of the plan – a square tower to each side
of a double passageway – can immediately be grasped. The
western opening was blocked at an early stage; its original
threshold, with a higher central stop for the double gate leaves,
is hardly worn. The blocking was removed by John Clayton. In
the eastern passage is a road surface of stone slabs at a higher
level, dating from late Roman times when this was the only
gate passage kept open on the north side of Hadrian's Wall.
The raised roadway contains pivot holes for the double doors
of the gate, and a stop block for them to close against. A big
rainwater drain, covered with slabs reused from earlier
structures, runs out through this portal.

North Gate

Hadrianic (AD 122–38)

Later Roman (AD 150–400)

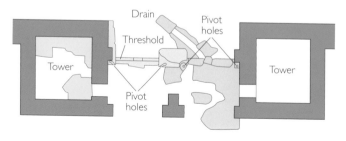

4

2 BARRACKS

The two most completely excavated barrack blocks in the north-east part of the fort face each other across a street, a recurrent arrangement in Roman forts. Each block could accommodate a *turma* or cavalry troop of about 30 men. Only the eastern halves have been excavated. The barracks that can be seen today probably date from the later second or early third century AD.

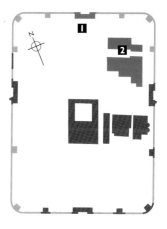

Each block consists of a row of rooms, a simple translation into permanent materials of the row of leather tents that would have been used on campaign. Until recently it was believed that the troopers lived in the barracks, with the horses stabled elsewhere. Recent discoveries at other Roman forts have now established that the barracks accommodated the horses too. Taking into account the unexcavated portion, the barracks were over 50m (164ft) long – providing sufficient space for ten rooms, each shared by three men and their horses.

Each of the rooms was divided into front and back parts. At Chesters the partitions are not visible today, but in two rooms of the northern barrack flagged walkways survive, leading from the front door to the position of a door in the partition, which led into the rear part. Three men slept and ate here. Their three horses were tethered in the front part, where an underfloor pit provided drainage.

The cavalryman had a deduction made from his annual salary – about one-fifth – to cover the cost of his horse, and he would have to pay this again if it was lost. This is one good reason why the mounts were kept where the troopers could keep a close eye on them, in combined 'stable-barracks'. There is evidence that each trooper had a slave who acted as a groom; the slave probably slept in the roof-space of the barrack.

Below: This complete quernstone for grinding grain was found in the barracks at Chesters. Such milling stones would have been used in the barracks by soldiers given the duty of preparing the bread ration for their troop

Bottom: A view looking east up the street that divided two of the barrack blocks

Right: Reconstruction of the barracks
in the north-east corner of the fort
at Chesters in about AD 200

A Stable area

B Living area

C Roof space

D Drain

E Colonnade

F Officer's house

At the rampart end, projecting into the street, is the house for the decurion, the officer in charge of the block. The functions of the individual rooms in the decurions' houses cannot be identified, but they would have included offices, rooms in which to sleep, dine and cook, and stables.

Surviving column bases show that a colonnade ran along the front of each barrack, offering cover for tethering or

Barracks

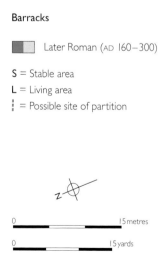

Later Roman (AD 160–300)

S = Stable area

L = Living area

⋮ = Possible site of partition

0 _____ 15 metres

0 _____ 15 yards

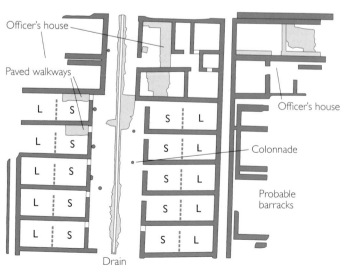

Officer's house

Paved walkways

Officer's house

Colonnade

Probable barracks

Drain

1 Decorative junction pieces slotted onto the straps of a horse's harness

2 Jointed snaffle bit from a horse's bridle

3 Fragment of a horse's decorative eyeguard found at Chesters

4 Fourth-century cavalryman's spur

5 Decorative mounts (*phalerae*), probably attached to a horse's harness

grooming horses in the open air. A big rainwater drain, which would also have helped disperse urine from the horses, runs along the centre of the street.

South of these barracks are the remains of a row of stone buildings, probably also barracks, but seemingly rebuilt during the course of the third or fourth century, resulting in a confused plan. Remains of late Roman rebuilds probably also existed over the main visible pair of barracks, but were either removed by 18th-century ploughing or without record during the 19th-century excavations.

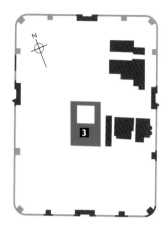

3 HEADQUARTERS (*PRINCIPIA*)

Occupying a central place in the fort, the headquarters or *principia* was both an administrative headquarters and the focus of loyal devotion to the standards of the regiment, to the gods, and to the emperor. The area of the Chesters *principia* is large in comparison with those also fully uncovered at other Wall-forts such as Housesteads, Vindolanda or South Shields. This reflects the prestige and status of the cavalry units. In all cases this was the most elaborate building in the fort.

The entrance on the north side of the building leads into a spacious paved courtyard. The bases of columns can be seen on two sides. These supported porticoes, or covered verandas. Gutters running along the edge of the courtyard collected the rainwater from their roofs. A well in the north-west corner was for ceremonial use; the main water supply for the fort was provided by an aqueduct. On a raised roundel on a flagstone near the well is an impressive carving of a phallus, a symbol of good luck.

Beyond the court is a *basilica*, or main hall. The foundations of an arcade define a northern aisle, entered by no fewer than five doors from the court and porticoes, and two further doors in its ends giving access from outside the building. Beyond the arcade, the enormous *basilica* would have had an eaves height of at least 10m (30ft). At the west end are the foundations of a platform (*tribunal*), originally some 2m (6ft) high, from which the commanding officer, or prefect (*praefectus*), would have presided over gatherings and ceremonies.

Above: *A phallus, a symbol of good luck, carved on a flagstone near the ceremonial well in the headquarters*

Right: *Reconstruction of the headquarters building in about* AD *200, from the south-west*

A Courtyard
B Porticoes
C Well
D Main hall (*basilica*)
E Platform (*tribunal*)
F Shrine (*aedes*)
G Strongroom

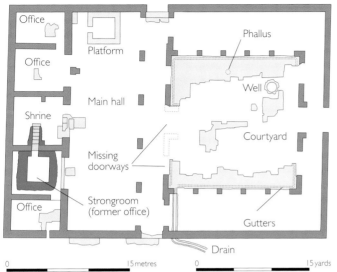

Headquarters

Hadrianic
(AD 122–38)

Later Roman
(AD 150–400)

Office

Platform

Office

Main hall

Shrine

Missing
doorways

Strongroom
(former office)

Office

Phallus

Well

Courtyard

Gutters

Drain

0   15 metres   0   15 yards

Opening off the back of the hall are five rooms. The pairs to either side are believed to have been the offices where the regimental records were kept and where pay was issued to troops, who could also bank savings there. The offices to either side of the central room had arched openings onto the hall (some voussoirs, or arch stones, lie about). These openings were closed by stone screens with grilles above, to form counters for transactions.

The central room (*aedes*) was a most sacred and revered shrine, constantly guarded. It contained the flag and standards of the unit and altars to the gods (including deified emperors). A statue of the living emperor is more likely to have stood in the *basilica* than in the *aedes* as often believed.

Above: *A dedication slab to the Emperor Antoninus Pius (AD 138–61) by the Sixth Legion Victrix, found in the south-east corner of the headquarters building at Chesters*

Right: Fragment from a monumental relief carving found in the headquarters building at Chesters. It originally depicted a standard-bearer, whose plumed helmet is just visible at the bottom. The inscription reads 'While the emperors are safe, fortunate is the Second Asturian Cavalry Unit'

Below: Aerial view of the headquarters building, looking north-east. The underground strongroom, with its vaulted roof, can be seen in the foreground

From the *aedes*, stairs led into an underground strongroom, or treasury, a later insertion that completely fills the office to the east of the *aedes*. The strongroom is one of the most remarkable survivals at Chesters, its vaulted roof still intact. When the chamber was finally cleared out shortly before 1840, it was found still to have its original wooden door covered with iron plates, riveted through with square nails. According to the antiquary John Hodgson, the door was 'sadly decayed' and soon disintegrated.

The standard plan of the military *principia* is highly reminiscent of the forum-*basilica* complex of a Roman city. For the Romans the city was the essential expression of civilization, and military encampments, auxiliary forts and legionary fortresses were all laid out in ways that recalled an ideal city plan. The second-century Roman army was a fighting force, but its buildings and rituals followed the patterns of Roman civic life.

Roman Military Religion

Inscribed altars, many examples of which can be seen in the museum, reveal that ordinary soldiers and high-ranking officers alike made sacrifices to the gods.

Two kinds of deities were worshipped by the soldiers. There were the official gods of the Roman state, including Jupiter, Juno, Minerva and Mars. Their statues and altars stood in the fort headquarters, and the same detailed calendar used by army units all over the empire laid down the occasions when these deities were to be honoured. The birthdays of long-dead emperors, who were deified after their death, were also celebrated.

Then there were the unofficial cults: those of native gods which remained local, or cults such as that of the popular Mithras, which spread through the army from distant parts of the empire. The Romans often identified local gods with their own, resulting in hybrids such as Apollo Maponus (from Britain) and Jupiter Dolichenus (from Syria). These unofficial cults had their own priests and temples which were usually outside the fort.

The headquarters was the centre of official religion. The prefect presided over the ceremonies, and among those soldiers excused menial tasks because of their specialist duties were priests (*haruspices*) who foretold the future from their inspection of the entrails of sacrificed animals.

Top: *Detail from Trajan's Column in Rome, erected in AD 113, showing the Emperor Trajan at an altar in his role as high priest, officiating at a sacrifice*

Right: *A fine statue of the goddess Juno Regina standing on a heifer, found at Chesters*

Left: *These miniature models of tongs, a bow and a spear, now in the Clayton Museum, would have been left by individual soldiers as votive offerings in temples and shrines*

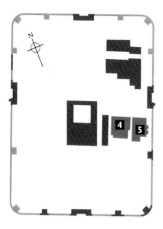

Below: Fragments of painted wall plaster found in the commanding officer's house (praetorium)

4 COMMANDING OFFICER'S HOUSE (*PRAETORIUM*)

In most auxiliary forts, the space to the right of the *principia* when looking towards the front of the fort (north at Chesters) was occupied by the commanding officer's house (*praetorium*). This was a peristyle house (that is, with a colonnaded courtyard at its centre) modelled on the sort of urban mansion that the commanding officer and his family would be used to in their Mediterranean city home. Inscribed tombstones and the writing tablets found at Vindolanda make it clear that such a prefect would have been accompanied by his wife, children and an extensive household of domestic staff and slaves.

At Chesters, however, the usual courtyard plan has been obscured by later structures. A complex of rooms can be seen, many with good examples of hypocaust (sub-floor) heating. It is possible that the small heated apartments belong

Commanding Officer's House and Baths

Later Roman (AD 150–400)

0 ————— 15 metres
0 ————— 15 yards

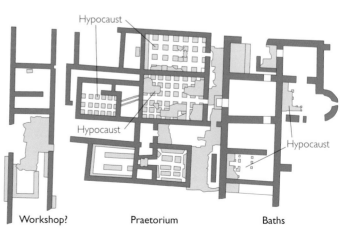

Hypocaust

Hypocaust

Hypocaust

Workshop?   Praetorium   Baths

Left: *The praetorium with the* praetorium *baths beyond, looking east towards the river. The pillars for hypocaust heating survive in several of the rooms of the* praetorium *and baths*

to a late period: fourth-century commanding officers were not always of the same social status as their predecessors, and sometimes their accommodation was comparatively small. Painted wall plaster from the *praetorium* at Chesters depicts a human face, a rare find for the Wall zone and a reminder of the rich decoration of the prefect's house.

The alpine fairy foxglove (*Erinus alpinus*) which grows on these walls was not planted by the Romans, as once romantically thought, but in John Clayton's time.

Above: *This copper-alloy crossbow brooch was found in the* praetorium *baths and dates to about* AD *350–80, when this building might have replaced the larger baths by the river*

Below: *Sculpture of a river god, probably representing the river North Tyne, found in the* praetorium *baths*

5 *PRAETORIUM* BATHS

To the east, separated from the heated rooms and partly shaded by a yew tree, is a free-standing bath building. This contains a section of raised hypocaust floor, supported on a combination of brick pillars and reused stone columns. This complex is traditionally described as the private baths of the commanding officer, but it is of considerable size and it seems more likely to have been for the soldiers, perhaps replacing the larger baths outside the fort at a late period; its excavation in the 1840s produced many fourth-century coins.

The positions of doorways are marked by threshold slabs with slots to either side. These held monolithic door frames, surviving examples of which can be seen at the baths outside the fort. This building was the find-spot in 1843 of a remarkable sculpture of a river god, perhaps representing the North Tyne.

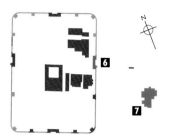

Right: Reconstruction of the east gate, looking south-west, as it might have appeared when first built under Hadrian in the AD 120s. The flat roofs with battlements represent one possible reconstruction. The proportions of the gate are reasonably certain, as the height of the semicircular gate arches can be established from the remains on site

⑥ EAST GATE

The east gate is the finest at Chesters and one of the best preserved on the whole of Hadrian's Wall. The two carriageway openings and flanking towers are clearly visible. At the back of the south passage, one side stands to its full original height, and a carved projecting impost shows the level from which the semicircular arch over the passage was sprung. From the height of the gate arches, which had a room above them, with the towers rising higher again, it is possible to calculate the minimum height of the original structure: it would have been some 3.5m (12ft) to the tops of the arches, and perhaps as much as 12m (40ft) to the tops of the towers. On the outside face of the south tower, Hadrian's Wall meets the fort south of the gate, so that both portals were on the north side of the Wall.

Above the unworn thresholds visible today was a secondary level with pivot stones for gate leaves. By about AD 300 the outer arches were walled up so that the interior of the gate could be converted into a set of rooms.

Below: View of the east gate, looking south-west

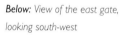

A Flanking towers

B Thresholds of carriageway openings

C Projecting impost for arch

D Pivot stones for gate leaves

E Hadrian's Wall

7 BATHS

Before their excavation in the 1880s the baths were buried by silt that had washed down the slope. As a result this is one of the best-preserved Roman military buildings in Britain. Baths normally stood outside the walls of auxiliary forts as they were not part of the standard fort plan, which was developed before the non-citizen auxiliaries adopted the custom of bathing in the late first century. The baths here have a distinctive compact plan only found at Wall-forts, and which belongs to the original building phase.

The changing room (*apodyterium*) is a hall spacious enough for athletic games. The seven niches in the west wall are a striking feature and were probably for bathers' clothes. Under the niches a carved stone bench support can be seen; this

Above: The remains of the baths looking north across the hot rooms
Below: Niches in the changing room, possibly for clothes

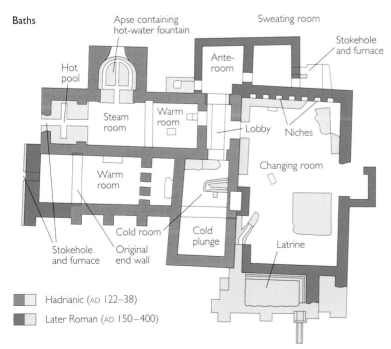

Baths

Apse containing hot-water fountain

Sweating room

Stokehole and furnace

Hot pool

Ante-room

Steam room

Warm room

Lobby

Niches

Warm room

Changing room

Cold room

Cold plunge

Latrine

Stokehole and furnace

Original end wall

Hadrianic (AD 122–38)

Later Roman (AD 150–400)

0   5 metres
0   5 yards

Below: These two fragments of small glass bottles found at Chesters would have contained scented oils or ointments. Bathers would have rubbed oils onto their skin after bathing

indicates the level of the original floor, buried by successive later resurfacings. In the south wall (just by the circular pillar-base) are the remains of a Roman lead water pipe. A communal latrine lies beyond the eastern end of the room.

A lobby leads from the changing room. To the left of it, the cold room (*frigidarium*) is not well preserved (note an opening into an underfloor drain); the cold plunge lay at the far end. To the right of the lobby an anteroom leads to the sweating room (*sudatorium* or *laconicum*). Here the heat ran up the walls behind a continuous jacket of stone slabs, a technique also seen in the internal baths. The furnace and stokehole are clearly seen from outside the building. The entry to the sweating room still has its monolithic stone door jambs. Thresholds slotted to take similar stone jambs can be seen elsewhere in the building (and in the *praetorium* baths): timber door frames would have warped in the steamy atmosphere.

Back in the lobby, steps made of arch-stones from the hollow overhead vaults descend into an oblong space. This

Roman Baths

Roman baths were essentially steam baths, rather like the modern Turkish bath (a direct descendant from the eastern Roman empire).

Heat was supplied by a furnace to the underfloor space (hypocaust). The hot gases ran under the floors, and were conducted up the walls through flues to be drawn out through vents at roof level, giving all-round radiant heat. Specially shaped stones were used to form arch-ribs which, combined with tiles, made a hollow vaulted ceiling.

By the second century AD an elaborate routine had evolved. The bather progressed from a changing area to the dry heat of a sweating room, and then, via a tepid room, to a steam room where hot water was sprinkled on the body and the dirt removed from the skin with a metal scraper (strigil). Here there was also a heated pool. Finally the bather returned to an unheated room and took a plunge in a cold pool.

Bathing was a social event. Bathers might compete in athletic and ball games beforehand, and in the baths themselves they would discuss business or gossip with friends. They also gambled – hence the tradition of erecting dedications to the goddess Fortuna in baths. Public baths were open to all, on payment of a small fee.

Above: Vaulting tubes (tubi fittili) used to create hollow vaulted ceilings
Left: Altar dedicated to the goddess Fortuna, found in the baths by the river at Chesters

was divided into a warm room (*tepidarium*) and steam room (*caldarium*). The raised floor, beneath which hot gases from the furnace circulated, and the supporting pillars, have vanished. The visitor walks at basement level, but threshold stones show the original floor level. In the *caldarium* is an apse, or projecting bay, which is likely to have contained a basin with a hot-water

Above: Key features of the baths

A Remains of the communal latrine

B The entry to the sweating room with its monolithic stone jambs

C Apse in the *caldarium* where a hot-water fountain stood

Elsewhere in the empire, men and women are known to have used the baths at the same time, although Hadrian is said to have passed a decree forbidding mixed bathing in Rome. Regulations on a second-century AD bronze tablet from the mining settlement of Vipasca in Portugal state that the baths were open to women in the morning and to men in the afternoon; there might have been similar arrangements in military communities.

Above: Reconstruction of the steam room and hot bath at Chesters in about AD 200. The apse to the right contained a hot-water fountain

Right: Box-tile found at Chesters, probably from the baths. Such tiles allowed hot air from the furnace to circulate up the walls of the warm and hot rooms of the baths

Above: Cutaway reconstruction of the hot rooms of the baths at Chesters in about AD 200

A Steam room

B Hot pool

C Apse containing the hot-water fountain

D Hypocaust

E Furnace and boiler

F Hollow vaulted ceiling

fountain. Still preserved is one of the few Roman windows to be seen in Britain (some of the window glass was found in the 1880s) and traces of pink waterproof cement lining the walls.

Over the criss-cross channels at the end of the *caldarium* stood the main hot immersion pool, entered through an arch, whose projecting side supports are visible. The lowest part of this opening would have been blocked at floor level by steps up to the bath. The hot pool lay, as always in Roman baths, immediately next to the furnace, which was outside the south wall of the building. The furnace supplied hot gases directly to the channels under the hot bath (and the hypocausts beyond), but also heated a suspended cylindrical boiler which fed the hot pool and the fountain. Water was probably supplied by an aqueduct diverted from the river upstream. The range to the east contained warm rooms through which the bather returned to the *frigidarium*.

Above: Fragments of window glass from the window in the apse of the steam room

Right: The apse of the steam room, with its central window, photographed shortly after excavation in 1884–5

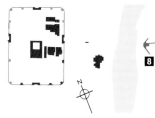

8 BRIDGE

A small section of Hadrian's Wall has been exposed to the north of the baths. From here, it is a short walk to a viewing platform overlooking the site of the west end of the Roman bridge. Much more can be seen of the bridge by following a path from the modern bridge at Chollerford (see map, page 3) to view the superb remains uncovered by John Clayton in the 1860s on the eastern side of the river.

The North Tyne has moved westwards since Roman times, leaving the eastern abutment (the masonry apron that projected into the river and protected the end of the bridge from the force of the water) high and dry. Conversely, the abutment on the fort side is now under water, but can sometimes be glimpsed when the river is low.

There are, in fact, remains of two successive bridges. Most of the visible masonry belongs to the second, larger bridge.

Above: This 1869 watercolour by David Mossman shows the recently excavated remains of the bridge at Chesters. The footings of the western abutment and two piers of the later bridge are shown under the water

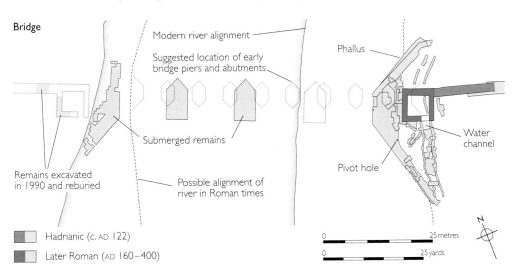

Bridge

Modern river alignment

Suggested location of early bridge piers and abutments

Submerged remains

Remains excavated in 1990 and reburied

Possible alignment of river in Roman times

Phallus

Water channel

Pivot hole

Hadrianic (c. AD 122)

Later Roman (AD 160–400)

0   25 metres
0   25 yards

Below: Reconstruction of the bridge at Chesters in the time of Hadrian, when it was designed to carry the Wall alone on nine narrow (4m wide) arches

Bottom: Reconstruction of the second bridge, built in the AD 160s. It was wide enough to carry the Military Way across the Tyne on four arches and had guard towers on each bank

The first, built under Hadrian, carried the Wall only, and was the same width as the originally planned Broad Wall: 3m, or 10 Roman feet. The lozenge shape of one of its piers, with cutwaters upstream and downstream, can be seen embedded in the later abutment. Its stones were locked together with dovetail-shaped clamps that are not used in the later bridge. The abutment of this early bridge was where the tower of the later bridge stands. The fact that the Wall bridges the river suggests that it had a walkway along its top: on the Continent, Roman frontier walls without walkways simply stopped when they reached rivers, and resumed on the other side.

The second bridge is now thought to date from the AD 160s, the time when the Military Way was built along the Wall. This bridge was correspondingly wider and more massive to carry the road, with a tower to guard it at each end. Many blocks from this bridge were surveyed and studied in 1982–3

and are displayed in a stone park on the east bank of the river. Some are from the decorative cornice that ran above the arches. These are heavily footworn and grooved, not for timbers, as was once thought, but for a stone parapet. This shows that the second bridge was also of stone, carrying the Military Way across the North Tyne on four graceful arches some 10m wide. The 18th-century Chollerford bridge, half a mile upstream, gives a good impression of the scale of its Roman predecessor. The Military Way was raised to the level of the bridge via a ramp (no longer visible). It is now known that the road ramp skirted the south sides of the towers rather than passing through them, as once thought. The parapet of the bridge was adorned with columns; the lower half of one lies on the abutment.

The abutment was constructed of massive unmortared blocks, locked together by tight jointing, iron clamps and continuous channels filled with molten lead. The Romans inherited this ancient construction technique from earlier civilizations; it is seen, for example, in the Parthenon. It is rarely encountered in Roman Britain and its use at Chesters shows that the bridge was a prestigious imperial building project. The rectangular slots in the top of many of the blocks are 'lewis holes' to take a lifting device so that the stones could be lifted into position by a crane. The pivot hole for the crane, 30cm (1ft) in diameter, is visible on the south wing of the abutment. On the face of the northern wing is a fine carving of a phallus, intended to ward off the destructive forces of the river.

At some date the southern wing of the abutment was extended southwards, with projecting toothed masonry to break up the force of the river. Later still, but within the Roman period, a massive water channel was driven through the tower and across the back of the abutment, possibly to drive a mill (as yet undiscovered) downstream.

Above: The bridge abutment on the east side of the North Tyne
Below: The antiquarian John Collingwood Bruce (1805–92), who published his first guide to Hadrian's Wall in 1851

'Next we meet with the most remarkable feature on the whole line of the wall – the bridge over the North Tyne.'
John Collingwood Bruce, *The Wallet-Book of the Roman Wall*, 1863

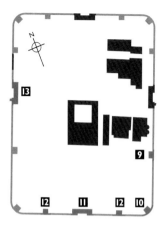

🆘 LESSER EAST GATE

Minor gates of this type are only found on Hadrian's Wall at forts which project beyond the barrier and were built because the main east and west gates were isolated on the north side of the Wall. This gate had only one portal and a single tower rising directly above. The paved surface runs outside the gate, where it becomes the Military Way and descends to the bridge via an embankment that is faintly visible, running to the left of the big tree that stands opposite the gate.

🔟 SOUTH-EAST ANGLE TOWER, 🆙 SOUTH GATE AND 🔢 INTERVAL TOWERS

The only internal structure now visible in the south part of the fort is a row of columns, probably marking the frontage of a south-facing barrack. On the southern fort wall the south-east angle (corner) tower, and two interval towers, filling the gaps between the corners and the centrally placed gate, can all be visited in sequence. Like the gate towers, these would have risen above the fort wall to a considerable height, perhaps 8m (25ft). On all other sides of the fort the remains of equivalent structures are still buried. The ground floors of such towers typically housed bread ovens or were used for storage. Sadly, at Chesters there are no detailed records of the Victorian excavations to breathe life into these impressive structures.

Below: The remains of the south-east angle tower

Bottom: The south gate was the main entry into the fort from the civilian settlement (vicus), which lay to the south of the fort

At the south gate the west passage was blocked early and consequently has an unworn threshold with a raised central door stop. To either side are the holes for the gate pivots. All trace of the blocking was removed by John Clayton. As at the north gate the eastern passage was kept open and contains the remains of two successive surfaces of blocks and slabs heavily worn by traffic. The uppermost surface has the usual pivot

The Chesters Diploma

This remarkable object, found at the south gate, is an inscribed bronze tablet issued in AD 145 to a retired soldier. After 25 years of service an auxiliary soldier was awarded Roman citizenship with the right to marry a non-citizen and pass on the citizenship to his descendants. This certificate confirmed his new status, and a copy was kept in Rome. Diplomas make it clear that, although serving soldiers were legally forbidden to marry, many in fact had 'unofficial' wives and families. Most diplomas were issued before AD 212, when citizenship was extended to virtually all free inhabitants of the empire.

Below: The Chesters Diploma, which is now in the British Museum. The Clayton Museum displays a replica

stones and door stop at a level almost 1m (3.2ft) higher than the Hadrianic pivot stones in the west portal, showing how the ground level in the fort rose over the centuries with successive rebuildings. Leaning against part of the upper surface is a fallen block, pierced with the holes for the upper ends of the gate pivots which turned to either side of the central pier. To either side of the passageways the towers are clearly seen. In the east tower the 'Chesters Diploma' was found (see feature above), an engraved bronze certificate awarding Roman citizenship to an auxiliary honourably discharged after 25 years' service.

⓭ WEST GATE

Returning along the west rampart, the lesser west gate, found directly opposite its eastern counterpart, is backfilled and no longer visible. At the west gate, as at the east, Hadrian's Wall joins onto the exterior of the south tower, leaving the two portals to open on the north side of the Wall. In the south portal, the original iron collars to contain the door pivots are still in place. Clayton found that both passages had been blocked. Heavy paving in the north passage dates from the

Below: Remains of an aqueduct which fed a tank in the north tower of the west gate

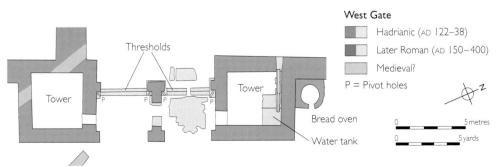

Thresholds

Tower

Tower

Bread oven

Water tank

West Gate

▢ Hadrianic (AD 122–38)

▢ Later Roman (AD 150–400)

▢ Medieval?

P = Pivot holes

0   5 metres

0   5 yards

23

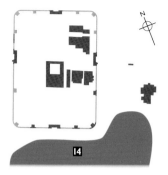

time when the passage interior had become a room. A channel enters the north tower of the gate from outside the fort; this is an aqueduct (probably not the principal one), which once fed a settling tank in the north-east corner of the tower. A bread oven is tucked into the angle of the north tower and fort wall. Two parallel stone walls diagonal to the south tower belong to a later structure built over the ruins of the gate. A short stretch of fort wall is exposed north of the gate; this brings the visitor to the north-west angle, and, following the rampart around, back to the north gate and the path to the museum.

14 CIVILIAN SETTLEMENT (*VICUS*)

It is worth pausing to look over the fence into the parkland south of the fort. There has never been any excavation here, but in drought conditions, the grass immediately above buried stone walls is starved of moisture, creating a pattern of 'parch marks', which are not visible from ground level, but show up in aerial photographs. These marks reveal the plan of the civilian settlement, or *vicus*, that flourished in the second and third centuries outside the walls of the fort.

The *vicus* covered an area much more extensive than the fort itself. It was filled with the 'strip buildings' usual in such settlements. These long structures, with their narrow ends facing onto the street frontages, were at a commercial premium, as their owners (or tenants; the premises probably being leased from the army unit) jostled to sell goods and services to the well-paid cavalrymen. There would also have been more elaborate buildings, such as an inn (*mansio*) for official travellers, and temples. Tombstones have been found in a secluded area by the river, south of the settlement, which suggests that this was the site of a cemetery.

Above: A bread oven in the angle of the north tower of the west gate and the fort wall. This is one of many that would have existed around the fort
Below: Engraving of the antiquary William Hutchinson (1732–1814) by Joseph Collyer the Younger, 1814
Below right: This aerial photograph taken during a severe drought in 1947 reveals roads and buildings of the vicus in the parched grass

'On the south side without the vallum and foss many ruins of buildings appear and some on the north.'
William Hutchinson, 1776

The People of the Wall

The soldiers of the Wall were perhaps outnumbered by civilian men, women and children.

With its well-paid and prestigious cavalry garrison, the fort and *vicus* formed a particularly large and vibrant mixed military and civilian community. It was closely linked, economically and culturally, to the Mediterranean world, receiving, for example, large quantities of olive oil in Spanish amphorae (pottery containers), and Samian pottery manufactured in Gaul.

A Diverse Community

The members of the *vicus* community had diverse origins. There is little evidence to suggest that they came in any significant numbers from the local native population: as with the fort, the style of building and the objects found in such settlements suggest an immigrant population, perhaps isolated from indigenous society. One inscription shows that a veteran lived at Chesters with his family. He was probably one of a sizeable community of veterans. A German named Lurio buried his sister, his wife and his son at Chesters; they must have lived in the *vicus*, as might families and dependants from the Spanish recruiting ground of *ala II Asturum* (Second Asturian Cavalry Unit).

There must have been priests of the many religious cults attested. An inscription from another Wall-fort mentions a society (*collegium*) of slaves. The majority of inhabitants were traders or craftsmen, perhaps originally from southern Britain, Gaul, or other parts of the empire from which trade networks extended to the northern frontier.

Above: Tombstone of Marcus Aurelius Victor, who died aged 50, from the cemetery at the edge of the vicus

Left: The owner of this Samian-ware pot found at Chesters inscribed the letters 'DIICIBA' – his name – Decebalus. Perhaps the pot's owner came from Dacia, modern-day Romania. Decebalus was also the name of the Dacian king depicted on Trajan's Column

Below: This leather shoe, mounted on a wooden foot by John Clayton's London bootmaker, was found in the ditch outside the south-east corner of the fort

Clayton Museum

AN ANTIQUARIAN DISPLAY

The Clayton Museum exhibits some of the most important 19th-century finds from the central section of Hadrian's Wall. The collection was largely made by John Clayton, who looks down from two portraits in the museum. From 1843, Clayton had begun a programme of land-purchase and excavation along a 20-mile length of the Wall, mostly west of Chesters. During his long life he acquired many Roman antiquities, through excavation, inheritance, gifts or purchase. Many of the items in the museum are therefore from sites other than Chesters, but in most cases the find-spot is known and given on a label, or on the plinths of the large stone objects. After Clayton's death in 1890 his nephew and heir, Nathaniel Clayton, commissioned the Newcastle architect, FW Rich, to build the museum.

With its hushed atmosphere, original glass cases and tiers of inscribed stones, the museum has an old-fashioned air: it has acquired historical value in its own right, and the Trustees of the Clayton Collection have been careful to retain its original style of display.

Top: A relief carving of three water nymphs found at Coventina's Well, a shrine at nearby Carrawburgh excavated by John Clayton in 1876. Many of the objects found in the shrine are now in the Clayton Museum

Above: Engraving of John Clayton's nephew Nathaniel George Clayton (1833–95), who commissioned the museum at Chesters

Left: These two red jasper gemstones were found at Chesters. They are engraved with (left) an image of Alexander the Great and (right) a woman's head

Facing page: An aisle in the main gallery of the Clayton Museum, with its ranks of altars and sculpture found at sites along the Wall

Above: The main gallery of the Clayton Museum, which retains its original cabinets and style of display
Below: Small personal objects from Chesters and elsewhere, now in the museum

A A belt buckle plate with a pattern of leaves

B Third- to fourth-century gilt copper-alloy circular brooch

C Silver-plated belt fitting with the letters 'VTER'. It was probably paired with a similar fitting on the other end of the belt, reading 'FELIX': together the two words read 'use happily'

D Double-sided bone hair comb with wide tines on one side and narrow tines on the other

E Copper-alloy bow brooch

F Handle of a knife depicting a dog chasing a hare

G Semicircular bone hair comb

THE COLLECTION
Life on the Wall

Many small items help us to picture the soldiers of Hadrian's Wall, their equipment and dress: finely decorated copper-alloy plates for decorating belts, strap-ends, brooches for fastening tunics, a sword hilt-guard, and pieces of sword-scabbards. The individual metal scales making up part of a suit of scale-armour would have been linked together, and there are fragments of helmets, including a carrying handle. There is also an extensive collection of pieces of horse-harness (see page 7), reminding us that Chesters was a cavalry fort.

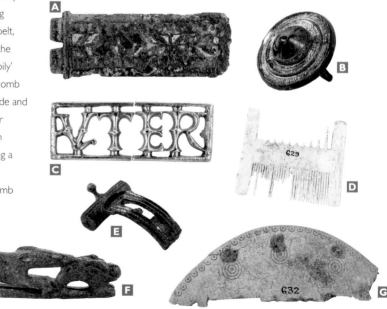

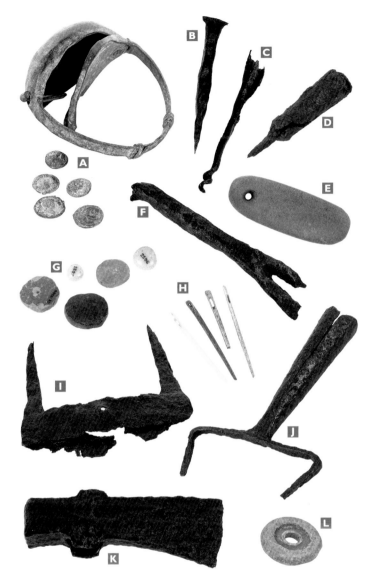

Left: Roman tools and personal objects from Chesters and elsewhere

A Bronze arm-purse and a collection of third-century silver coins

B Chisel, perhaps for metal-working

C Gimlet for boring holes in wood

D Awl for punching holes in wood or leather

E Small whetstone

F Wrecking bar

G Gaming counters, used on gridded gaming boards

H Bone needles

I Spade sheath (the spade itself would have been made of wood with the metal wrapped around)

J Pitchfork

K Axe

L Spindle whorl used to weigh down a distaff to spin wool

Below: Personal objects from Chesters and elsewhere, which were more likely to have belonged to women

A Bone hairpins with decorated heads

B Delicate gold chain from a necklace or bracelet

C Glass and jet beads

Gaming counters, needles for darning and whetstones for sharpening implements and weapons show how off-duty time might have been passed, while arm-purses contained the coins which the well-paid soldier would have taken to spend in the shops, taverns, jewellers and craft workshops of the *vicus*.

As well as being warriors, Roman soldiers were builders and specialist craftsmen, and this is amply illustrated by a wide variety of tools such as leather- and wood-working implements, awls, picks, axes, masons' trowels, chisels and wrecking bars. The museum contains a pitchfork, probably from Chesters, which we can imagine the cavalrymen or their grooms using to move the hay for their horses. There has been no excavation in the civilian *vicus* at Chesters, so most of the Chesters items came from inside the fort. The same is true of a range of objects associated with women: hairpins, bracelets and beads, a reminder that Roman forts were not an all-male environment, with women – whether soldiers' relatives, civilians from the *vicus*, or slaves – always present.

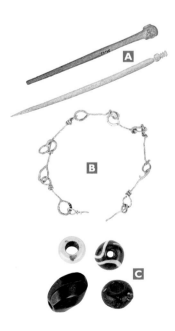

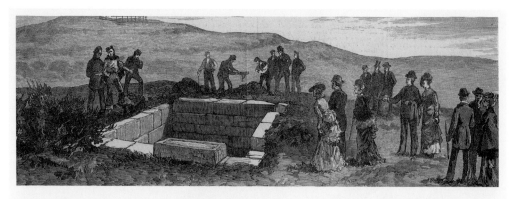

Coventina's Well

The museum contains many of the finds from Coventina's Well, found by chance in 1876 at the next Wall-fort to the west, Carrawburgh, and excavated by Clayton.

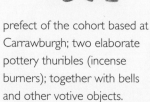

The 'well' was the stone lining of a natural spring, enclosed in a temple sacred to a water nymph, Coventina, whose name also occurs in Spain and Gaul. Worshippers came to make offerings at the shrine throughout the history of Hadrian's Wall. Over 13,000 coins had been thrown into the sacred spring. Most are now in the British Museum. At least

3,000 more coins disappeared at the time of discovery: 'In the peaceful and well-ordered county of Northumberland … such a raid could not have been anticipated', Clayton wrote at the time.

It is not known for certain what Coventina's powers were supposed to be, but she was probably a healing deity. Offerings of coins continued to be thrown into the well as late as the AD 380s, important evidence for the continuation of pagan religion on Hadrian's Wall at a time when the empire was increasingly Christian.

At the end of the fourth century the shrine was finally destroyed and its accumulated paraphernalia thrown into the well. This included over 20 altars, eight of them inscribed; a stele depicting the goddess, dedicated by the

prefect of the cohort based at Carrawburgh; two elaborate pottery thuribles (incense burners); together with bells and other votive objects.

Top: Victorian visitors viewing the exavated shrine, in an engraving for the Illustrated London News, *1876*
Above: *This figurine of a horse, found in the well, has a stud on the back, suggesting that it was originally attached to something*
Left: *A slab dedicated to 'the goddess Coventina' showing her reclining on a river bank, holding an aquatic plant*
Below: *One of two elaborately decorated thuribles found at Coventina's Well*

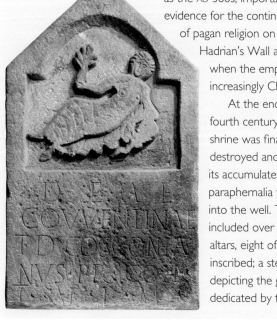

Left: An impressive relief carving of the god Mars, which probably adorned the entrance to the principia building at Housesteads, is now in the Clayton Museum

Below: An ornate jet finger ring with Christian symbols and an inscription that translates as 'who shall separate mine and thine while life lasts?'

Bottom: A humble altar from Chesters, set up by Tertulus to the non-Roman god Vitiris. This deity is only known in the north of England and seems to have been popular with soldiers in the third century

Gods All Around

Visitors will immediately be struck by the number of stone altars in the museum, used to make offerings to the bewildering range of pagan gods, official or unofficial, overseas or local, that played a big part in the lives of the people of the Wall. A large and beautiful altar from Vindolanda was dedicated by a prefect from Brescia in Italy (Brixia on the inscription) to Jupiter, head of the Roman pantheon. Mars, the god of war, appears on a big relief at the entrance to the museum which once adorned the headquarters building at Housesteads.

A headless female figure standing on the back of a heifer (see page 11) creates a striking impression. Of outstanding sculptural quality by the standards of the northern frontier, she is the goddess Juno Regina, consort of the sky god Jupiter Dolichenus, who would have been depicted standing on a bull in an accompanying statue, of which only the base remains. The cult originated at Doliche in modern Turkey, and by the third century was widespread among the army.

31

Top: Sandstone arch from the shrine of Mars Thincsus at Housesteads

Above: *An over life-size solid bronze hand. Heavy restoration makes it difficult to tell whether or not it was originally attached to a statue – it might have been a votive offering*

Below: *A fragment from a fine glass vessel painted with the design of a fish, found at Chesters*

Right: *A Samian-ware bowl stamped 'IOENALIS', the name of a maker who was producing pots in central Gaul between about AD 100 and 130*

The Roman habit of identifying local Celtic or German gods with their own is illustrated by a tall dedication to Mars Thincsus, a conflation of Mars with a German war god. This stone is one side of a doorway giving entry to a temple found at Housesteads in 1883. The arched head of the doorway can be seen above, with Mars Thincsus accompanied by a goose (symbol of aggression, and therefore war). The dedicators named are members of one of many irregular Germanic mounted units posted to the Wall in the third century. Other objects include votives – offerings that would have been placed in temples – like the miniature bow, spear and smith's tongs (see page 11) and an above life-size human hand, and lamps and bells used in the ceremonies in such shrines.

Trade and Supply

Of the traded goods (such as textiles or foodstuffs) that came from many parts of the empire, few traces survive except for pottery and glass, which does not rot away in the ground. Lustrous red-orange Samian ware from Gaul can be closely dated and the museum has many examples of the various standard forms, often bearing a tiny stamp with the potter's

The Carvoran Modius

This important object, now in the Clayton Museum, is a bronze corn measure, found by a postman on his round at the Wall-fort of Carvoran in 1915. The inscription states that it holds 17.5 *sextarii* (equivalent to about 9.5 litres), but in fact it holds rather more. Some think that this discrepancy was to defraud Britons paying tax in corn, but it is more likely that the modius was used for issuing rations (wheat for men, barley for horses), not to individual soldiers but to each century or cavalry troop. The wheat would be ground using milling stones (querns) like the complete example found at Chesters (see page 5), and bread baked in a communal oven that lay close by each barrack block (one can be seen by the west gate of the fort – see page 24).

name, or inscribed with ownership marks. Grit-studded mixing bowls (*mortaria*), a colour-coated 'hunt cup' from the Nene Valley, near Peterborough, and less glamorous 'coarsewares' were all supplied from production centres in Britain. The museum also has a fragment of a cylindrical painted glass vessel depicting a fish, imported from the Rhineland, and late Roman engraved glass of high quality.

Running an Empire

Britain was organised as a province on exactly the same lines as every other province in an empire that had triumphed through the practical Roman genius for administration. Written information, compiled and communicated by military and civil officials, was vital to this. A Samian-ware inkwell in the museum is evidence of a world where voluminous written records were kept. The province was controlled via a system of roads along which troops and officials could travel rapidly. The museum contains a remarkable group of inscribed cylindrical milestones from the Stanegate, the road running south of the Wall between Corbridge and Carlisle (one of the stones measures 14 miles from Corbridge). Even the soldiers building Hadrian's Wall left a written record of their work: the museum contains many so-called 'centurial stones'. One names the centurion Lousius Suavis, who recorded the work of his troops at no fewer than six different places along the Wall. Overall responsibility for the smooth running of the province lay with the governor, the emperor's personal representative (*legatus augusti*). The name of one governor of Britain, Ulpius Marcellus (AD 178–84), can be seen on an inscription recording the construction of an aqueduct with the words *aqua adducta* (see page 41).

Above: The Carvoran Modius, an official vessel for measuring grain rations. In the inscription, the name of the Emperor Domitian (r.AD 81–96) has been erased in 'damnatio memoriae', the process whereby all traces of an unpopular or discredited individual were destroyed

Below: This copper-alloy box with enamel decoration protected a wax seal, and was perhaps attached to important documents

Bottom: A centurial stone recording the building of a stretch of Hadrian's Wall by centurion Lousius Suavis and his men, found near Chesters

History of Chesters

THE CONQUEST OF BRITAIN

The Emperor Claudius invaded Britain in AD 43, but 80 years were to elapse before another emperor, Hadrian, built a frontier wall across the island. Conquest was slow and the creation of a pacified province took time. The army did not penetrate northern Britain until AD 70. The high tide of conquest came with a victory in Scotland in AD 83. Roman forts extended all the way to the Scottish highlands, and it seemed as if the whole of Britain lay within Rome's grasp. But after AD 85 a series of barbarian invasions on the Danube frontier made it necessary to withdraw troops from Britain. Scotland was abandoned. By AD 105 the Romans had given up the last remaining forts north of the narrow neck of land between the rivers Tyne and Solway. More forts were built along this line and it was consolidated into a military frontier.

On his accession in AD 117 Hadrian inherited severe problems left over from aggressive wars waged by his predecessor, Trajan (r.AD 98–117). Hadrian responded by keeping the empire within its bounds and securing its frontiers to protect the provinces. He toured the frontiers, visiting Britain (probably in AD 122), and the idea of fortifying the Tyne–Solway isthmus with a Wall may well have been his own.

Above: *Hadrian addresses the army of Britain. This rare coin belongs to a series dedicated to the armies of the frontier provinces*
Below: *The central section of Hadrian's Wall, looking east towards Broomlee Lough*

Facing page: *A larger than life-size head of the Emperor Hadrian. It is the only portrait of the emperor to have been found in Britain, and was probably made here*

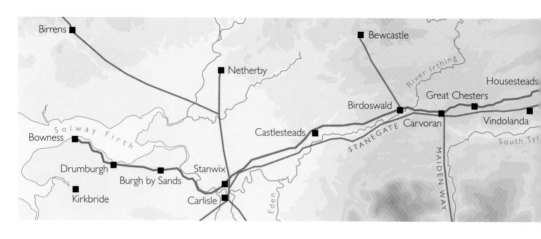

*Above: Milecastle 39, to the west
of Housesteads*

*Below: Hadrian's Wall was built by
legionary soldiers. This centurial stone,
now in the Clayton Museum, records
the construction of a short stretch of
the Wall by centurion Flavius Civilis
and his men*

BUILDING HADRIAN'S WALL

The original plan was for a stone wall 10 Roman feet (3m)
wide and perhaps some 20 Roman feet (6m) high, fronted by
a great ditch. The Wall was to cut ruthlessly in long straight
stretches across the countryside. Only on the higher ground of
the crags in the central sector did it snake about to follow the
cliff-tops. The only troop accommodation was to be in the
form of small forts at mile intervals – 'milecastles'. Regularly
spaced between every two milecastles were two watchtowers
(known as 'turrets'). The Wall was to be 80 Roman miles long,
the western 31 miles being built of turf.

Construction began in about AD 122, the work being
undertaken by the three legions based in Britain. Within a year
or two there was a change of plan. For some reason – possibly
warfare triggered by the building of the Wall – it was necessary
to add forts manned by non-citizen auxiliary units to the line
itself. There were at first 15 forts along the line of the Wall.
The earliest to be added were built straddling the Wall, with
three of the main gates lying on the north side and only one
to the south. Whatever had been built of the Wall and its
structures had to be demolished, and the ditch filled, to
make way for the forts. Two other changes came with the
addition of the forts. The width of the Wall was narrowed to
8 Roman feet (2.4m) or less. A ditch, flanked by mounds
– known as the Vallum – was dug to the south, marking the
rear of the Wall corridor.

Shortly after Hadrian's death in AD 138 his successor,
Antoninus Pius (r.AD 138–61), decided to invade Scotland once
more, and to fortify the Forth–Clyde isthmus with a wall of
turf. It is not really known how thoroughly Hadrian's
Wall was decommissioned at this time. The Antonine
Wall in Scotland was short-lived: the Romans gave it up
after only about 20 years. By AD 160 Hadrian's Wall had
been re-occupied and the turf section was being rebuilt
in stone. The Wall would remain the northern frontier
of Britain until the Romans abandoned the province
some two and a half centuries later.

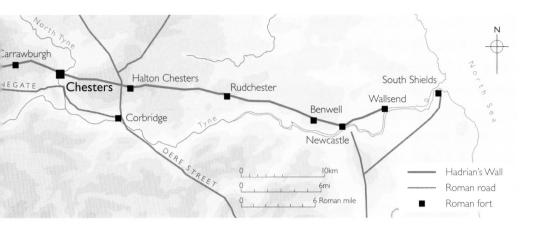

WHAT THREATS DID THE WALL FACE?

Some archaeologists believe that the Wall's main functions were to regulate trade and immigration, collect customs, and detect bandits. But this does not explain why it was a defensible barrier, the most elaborate of all the frontier walls the Romans ever built. The Wall seems to have been more than a mere statement of imperial grandeur – it was intensively manned, repaired and maintained for nearly three centuries. One Roman historian records that a hostile invasion succeeded in penetrating the Wall shortly after AD 180, implying that it was intended to prevent such incursions. Although it was not meant to withstand siege, the Wall could effectively hinder and help intercept both minor raids and larger barbarian invasions. We have no records of day-to-day operations on the Wall, but an inscription noted at Hexham Abbey in 1725 records that a cavalry unit, probably the *ala II Asturum* (Second Asturian Cavalry Unit) of Chesters, had 'wiped out a host of Corionototae' – an otherwise unknown but clearly hostile people.

Above: Map of Hadrian's Wall, which ran for 73 miles across the north of Britain

Below: Diagram showing the development of Hadrian's Wall

A AD 100 Stanegate, a road linking Roman forts between the Tyne and the Solway

B AD 125 First plan of Hadrian's Wall and ditch

C AD 130 The Vallum is built south of the Wall; Wall width reduced from 10 to 8 Roman feet or less

D AD 180 The Military Way, linking the forts, is built between the Wall and the Vallum

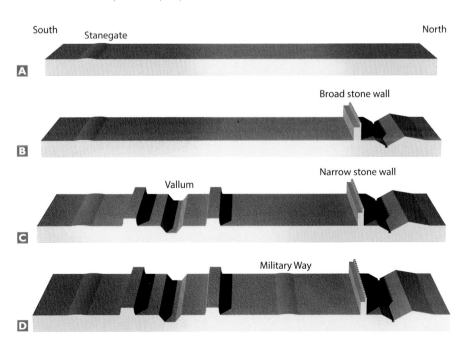

Roman Cavalry

Roman cavalry units were made up of auxiliary soldiers who excelled in fighting on horseback, and were recruited from across the empire.

Although legionaries (citizen troops) built the Wall and its forts, the nearest legionary base was at York. The units stationed at Chesters and elsewhere on the Wall were auxiliaries. These non-citizens were originally recruited from warrior peoples that Rome had encountered in her frontier wars. They were valued for military skills which the legions lacked, such as fighting on horseback.

Auxiliaries were organized into cohorts of infantry and *alae* – 'wings' – of cavalry (and many mixed units), mostly 500 strong. From the beginning Chesters was base to an *ala* of cavalry, the most prestigious and highly paid kind of unit in the auxiliary army.

In the early empire a 500-strong *ala* consisted of 16 troops (*turmae*) of about 30 horsemen, each led by a decurion (equivalent to an infantry centurion). Unlike the legions, auxiliary units were not commanded by men of the highest senatorial class. The *ala* was in the charge of a prefect, typically a young Roman aristocrat of the equestrian order, from a city in the Mediterranean lands, who took up the post as part of his progress through the ranks of the imperial service.

Cavalry Equipment

The standard equipment for patrols and military operations included helmet, mail armour, a sword and spears. The rider had no stirrups; he was held firmly in place by four pommels at each corner of the saddle. The decorated harnesses and trappings for his horse can be reconstructed from depictions in sculpture and finds of the metal connecting parts

(see examples on page 7). Horseshoes were not used on cavalry horses.

When arrayed for their training exercises, wearing masked helmets with the faces of gods and mythological figures, the horsemen of an *ala* must have been one of the most spectacular sights of the ancient world.

Top: Reconstruction of auxiliary cavalry on parade wearing helmets like the one above
Above: *Roman cavalry parade helmet found at Crosby Garrett, Cumbria*

THE FOUNDATION OF CHESTERS

There has not been enough modern excavation for us to know if there was any pre-Roman settlement at Chesters. At present the story begins in AD 122 with Hadrian's Wall, laid in a straight east–west course across the site, and the building of a bridge to carry the Wall across the North Tyne. When the decision was taken, probably in about AD 124, to build a fort, the Wall ditch was filled and a recently built turret (27a) demolished. Its remains (not visible) were found in 1945 outside the north-east corner of the headquarters.

The defences and principal buildings were built of stone. An inscription of Hadrianic date found in the bank of the North Tyne as recently as 1978 shows that the unit stationed in the new fort was the 500-strong *ala Augusta ob virtutem appellata* – 'the cavalry unit named Augusta on account of its courage'. This unit would have required 16 stable-barracks, which were probably made of timber. Nothing is known of their plan, as excavation has never gone deep enough to reach these early levels, but it is likely that eight barracks lay in the front part of the fort and eight in the rear.

Above: Altar dedicated to 'the discipline of the Emperor Hadrian by the cavalry unit named Augusta'. Found at Chesters in 1978, it shows the name of the first unit, the *ala Augusta,* to occupy the fort

THE DEVELOPMENT OF THE FORT

The only time in its history that Chesters might not have been a cavalry fort was during the confused years of the mid second century. It is uncertain whether Chesters was fully occupied while the Antonine Wall in Scotland was held (AD 142–60). At some point in the reign of Antoninus Pius legionaries carried out a programme of building work. A building inscription,

The Changing Layout of Chesters (conjectural)

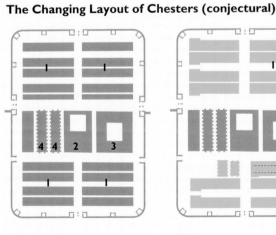

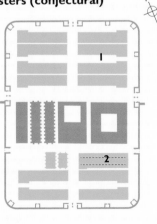

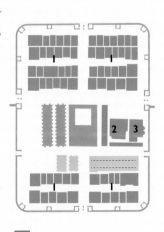

AD 122

The fort as first built with barracks **1**, the headquarters (*principia*) **2**, the commanding officer's house (*praetorium*) **3**, and granaries **4**

AD 180–250

The excavated barracks **1** date from this phase. The aisled building **2** may have been a drill hall

AD 300

The barracks **1** are now broken up into separate units as is the *praetorium* **2**, with the *praetorium* baths **3** alongside it

Above: Reconstruction of Chesters fort and vicus in about AD 180, looking south

A North gate

B Barracks

C Headquarters (*Principia*)

D Commanding officer's house (*Praetorium*)

E Granaries

F Possible drill hall

G Baths

H Bridge

I Vallum

J Military Way

K South gate

L Civilian settlement (*Vicus*)

probably of the period AD 138–80, was left here by an auxiliary unit, *cohors I Delmatarum* (First Cohort of Dalmatians). It is unclear whether or not this infantry unit was stationed here on any more than a temporary basis while carrying out building work. A commander of a further auxiliary unit, the First Cohort of Vangiones (raised in the Rhineland) buried his daughter at Chesters. Her tombstone dates to after AD 160, but it is uncertain whether this unit was ever based at the fort.

An inscription naming Ulpius Marcellus, the governor of Britain in AD 178–84, confirms that by this time the fort was once again the base of a cavalry unit, *ala II Asturum*. The Asturians, originally raised in northern Spain, were to have a long association with Chesters, remaining there until the end of the Roman period.

The visible barracks are part of a complete rebuilding of the accommodation of *ala II Asturum*, probably in the later second or early third century. There was not room inside the fort for 16 of these new barracks, suggesting that the number of subdivisions (*turmae*) of the *ala* was reduced to 12 or 14 by the early third century. At other forts on Hadrian's Wall in the third century, irregular units of Germanic barbarians supplemented the old auxiliary units; at Chesters a recently discovered inscription of AD 286 possibly refers to *symmacharii* (allied

irregular troops). In the third century, former barrack space was sometimes taken up by other kinds of buildings: an aisled structure appearing in the southern part of the fort on the Victorian plan could just possibly be a cavalry drill hall.

As at all Roman forts in northern Britain, the period AD 180–250 was the heyday of the civilian settlement lying outside the fort walls, as military pay, and buying power, were increased. In these years all such external settlements or *vici* reached their greatest prosperity and extent. The vast majority of the inscriptions from the site date to this time, recording building projects, declarations of loyalty to the emperor, religious ceremonies, and burial of the dead.

Left: Inscription from Chesters recording an aqueduct (aqua adducta) erected by the auxiliary cavalry unit, the ala II Asturum, at the time when Ulpius Marcellus was governor of Britain (AD 178–84)

Above: Copper-alloy coins, or nummi, found at Chesters. All date from between AD 324 and 350. The coin on the left shows two soldiers holding standards

Below: A medieval manuscript copy of the Notitia Dignitatum, a Roman document recording the presence of ala II Asturum at Chesters at the end of the Roman period. The island of Britain is depicted on the left, with the Hadrian's Wall garrisons listed on the right

THE THIRD AND FOURTH CENTURIES

An absence of written sources means that we know little about events in Britain during the third century, but elsewhere the years AD 230–70 were a time of dire crisis, as civil wars and barbarian invasions destroyed the traditional structure of the Roman army and severed many of the links between the provinces and the Mediterranean. By the fourth century the *ala* at Chesters was completely rooted in its locality, its manpower drawn above all from the sons of serving soldiers, since hereditary service had become compulsory in the late empire. By AD 300 the traditional Roman practice of carving inscriptions had mostly ceased in Britain (with the exception of a few tombstones and milestones), so we have no written records of the history or daily life of fourth-century Chesters. Materially the soldiers were much poorer than their high-imperial predecessors, and there are fewer finds from this period. The soldiers were increasingly paid in kind (foodstuffs and clothing), but still received some cash payments; coins were still widely used.

Despite these changes, the same regiment seems to have garrisoned the fort as before: the *Notitia Dignitatum*, a list of civil service posts and military commands throughout the Roman empire compiled in the early fifth century, lists the Wall garrisons, and still places *ala II Asturum* at Chesters. The barracks inside the fort were probably extensively altered and rebuilt in the fourth century, but no records were kept during the Victorian excavations of any late structures that might have been removed to expose the visible barracks. It is not possible to reconstruct a detailed plan of the fort in the fourth century.

Two additional granaries in the southern part of the fort, however, were presumably in use in this period (if not earlier),

and the late fort plan could have accommodated 12 barracks for 12 *turmae* (about 360 horsemen). There is therefore no reason to think that before AD 350 the garrison was drastically reduced in numbers from its third-century level, as has sometimes been suggested.

Although there has been no excavation of the civilian settlement at Chesters, evidence from other forts in the north suggests that by the end of the third century the *vicus* would have been completely abandoned. In the late Roman period, rather than being permanently attached to the unit as they had been in the third-century *vici*, traders travelled to periodic markets held within the fort walls. This is indicated by areas of high-intensity fourth-century coin loss found in some recently excavated forts. The only late Roman civilian population centres that we know of in the Wall area are the towns of Carlisle and Corbridge (the last only a very short journey from Chesters). By the early AD 300s, settlement at Chesters was thus confined within the fort walls, with only fields outside (whether cultivated by soldiers or civilians living in the fort, we do not know). Even the baths were perhaps now abandoned and replaced by the *praetorium* baths inside the fort.

CHESTERS IN THE FIFTH CENTURY

In the early fifth century, Britain passed out of the administrative control of a Roman empire that was weakened by civil wars and barbarian invasions on the Continent. The unit at Chesters had probably dwindled in size and become increasingly cut off from central authority for several decades. It is uncertain whether the last remnants were removed to serve elsewhere, or whether they were left to fend for themselves. There is increasing evidence for occupation in the Wall-forts for much of the fifth century and possibly beyond, but it is far from certain that the inhabitants were descendants of the last Roman soldiers to be based there.

Above: A stokehole and part of the hypocaust of the *praetorium* baths within the fort walls. By the fourth century these baths had probably superseded the earlier building by the river

Below: A number of small objects from Chesters, now in the museum, show that the fort was still being occupied in the fourth and fifth centuries

A A crossbow brooch dating from about AD 340–380

B Jet beads, probably dating from the fourth century

C A ring-headed pin for fastening clothes, dating from the fourth or fifth century

Above: Part of the Saxon crypt at Hexham Abbey, which was built reusing stones taken from Corbridge and from the Roman bridge at Chesters

AFTER THE ROMANS

Whatever after-life there was among the ruins, there was never again a major settlement at Chesters. In about AD 675 Saxon builders came to the site to dismantle the remains of the Roman bridge over the North Tyne to obtain building materials for the church and crypt built by Wilfrid at Hexham. Otherwise the site was absorbed into an agricultural estate, although the ruins of the fort must have been upstanding enough to prevent the site from being ploughed for many centuries. The nave of Chollerton church, two miles north-east, built in about 1200, has an arcade of four Roman monolithic columns, presumably brought from Chesters. Gradually agriculture encroached on the ruins, but the site was still being quarried for its ready-dressed stone as late as the 18th century.

Accounts by visitors to the fort in the 18th century (when it was known as 'Walwick Chesters') describe the site before it was levelled by ploughing and later landscaping. When he visited in the 1720s, the antiquary John Horsley saw 'large ruins' inside the fort, and could make out the *vicus*. In 1760 Bishop Pococke was shown 'a cavity called Adam's Garden, which they told me was lately discovered and was arched over'. William Hutchinson, 16 years later, saw the *vicus* and described the street plan inside the fort. This allows the still visible ridge and furrow ploughing, which obscured the streets he described, to be dated to after 1776.

An Eventful Visit

In 1801 the Reverend John Skinner (1772–1839) visited Chesters during a walking tour along the Wall. His diary notes 'large masses of ruins' at the site, but also records the hazards facing a lone

traveller: 'I must remark … that civility to strangers by no means appears to be a characteristic of the people of Northumberland … At one cottage … close to the Wall, I saw a woman at her door with a sheep-dog by her side and as I approached … she shut herself in the house and endeavoured to set the dog on me; had I not been armed with a stick, in all probability I might have been bitten. At Chesters … it was not much better, for the farmer who was in the field with his reapers did not attempt to call off his dog when he was running to me, and it was some time before I could persuade him that my intentions were pacific

in visiting these parts. How absurd is the idea of Arcadian simplicity and benevolence in the lower orders.'

Above: Portrait of John Skinner, rector of Camerton, Somerset, by an unknown artist
Left: Sketch of the Juno Regina statue and other inscriptions at Chesters from John Skinner's notebook, 1801

JOHN CLAYTON AND CHESTERS

In 1796 Nathaniel Clayton bought the estate. He had the ruins levelled and grassed over to form a park between his mansion and the river. His son John Clayton succeeded to the property in 1832.

John Clayton is one of the most important figures in the 19th-century archaeology of Hadrian's Wall. He was a lawyer and for many years was the influential town clerk of Newcastle. He was fascinated by Roman antiquity, and carried out a programme of excavations in his grounds at Chesters over many years. He also acquired as many other sites in the central sector of the Wall as he could, and had a number of them excavated. The fort at Housesteads, and the lengths of exposed grass-topped curtain wall, partly rebuilt, which run along the crags of the Whin Sill, owe their present appearance to Clayton's workmen. In obtaining these sites Clayton rescued them from quarrying, stone robbing and destruction by farming. Clayton devoted every Monday to excavation, starting at Chesters with the commanding officer's house and internal baths in 1843. He was still excavating just before his death in 1890. Clayton's chief workmen were William Tailford, who died in about 1860, and Tailford's son, also named William, who dug at Chesters for 45 years.

After 1890 Clayton's nephew and heir, Nathaniel George Clayton, continued the work, excavating the barracks. He built the museum which houses the store of antiquities amassed by John Clayton. The present mansion, glimpsed through trees to the west of the fort, owes its form to Nathaniel George. The current appearance of the Roman site, with its disinterred

Above: Watercolour painting of the east gate at Chesters in 1869, by David Mossman. This is the earliest known depiction of the east gate
Below: Portrait photograph of John Clayton taken in about the 1840s

Right: The summer house in the
garden of his mansion at Chesters
was used by John Clayton to house
some of his many antiquities
Below: Detail from a watercolour
sketch by Thomas Miles Richardson
Junior, of about 1843, showing
some of the carved stones, ceramics,
and other antiquities discovered
at Chesters
Bottom: Photograph from the early
1890s showing the excavated
remains of the barracks at Chesters,
looking north-west. Animal bones and
other objects discovered during the
excavation were left on display

fragments separated by large unexcavated areas, is entirely the
product of the Claytons; there has been hardly any digging
since the death of Nathaniel George in 1895. The estate
passed out of the Clayton family in 1929.

The fact that almost all the visible remains at Chesters
were unearthed between 1843 and 1895 means that there is
much about them that today cannot be understood, by trained
archaeologist and casual visitor alike. This is because at that time
there was only a limited concept of archaeological stratigraphy.
Where a modern archaeologist would try to understand how
the layers and structures on the site had built up over time, the
Victorian excavators simply dug until they reached remains
solid enough to display, collecting any spectacular finds along
the way. Hardly any systematic record was kept of the
excavations or of what was removed. Only at the site of the

A Family of Collectors

The museum at Chesters is not just the work of a single individual, but reflects the efforts of a remarkable family of antiquaries and collectors.

John Clayton's maternal grandmother, Bridget Atkinson (1730–1814), collected coins, as well as shells from all over the world. Bridget's antiquarian interests were clearly well regarded by her contemporaries: she was made an honorary member of the Society of Antiquaries of Newcastle-upon-Tyne when it was founded in 1813. This was highly unusual, especially as women were not allowed to become full members of the society until the 1870s.

Her daughter Jane was given Roman coins, pottery and other objects discovered when repairs were being made to the bridge at Kirkby Thore, Cumbria. These, together with her mother's coins and shells, entered the Clayton Collection. The collection also includes

Roman coins acquired by one of John Clayton's sisters, Sarah-Anne (1795–1880). John noted that his sister had a keen eye for reading Roman inscriptions and would sometimes help him to interpret new discoveries.

John Clayton's nephew and heir, Nathaniel George Clayton, built the museum at Chesters, which opened in 1896. His son John Bertram (1861–1900) ran the museum for the first few years. After John Bertram's death, his mother, Isabel (1840–1928), kept the museum open to the public, allowed excavations on her land, and even employed an archaeologist to care for the remains. The Clayton Collection and Museum, as well as much of the central section of Hadrian's Wall, stand as a lasting legacy to the efforts of John and his wider family.

Top: Photograph taken of the newly constructed museum in about 1900, built to house the Clayton Collection
Above: *Portrait engraving of Bridget Atkinson*
Below: *These huge clam shells are on display in the museum. They were collected by Bridget Atkinson, who sourced shells from around the world: she even enlisted the help of the purser on Captain Cook's third voyage (1776–80) to seek new specimens*

Above: Looking west across the north gate towards the river North Tyne

Below: Ceramic flagon decorated with a woman's face, found by John Clayton at Coventina's Well. In 2016 English Heritage carried out a major refurbishment of the museum at Chesters, safeguarding Clayton's collection for future generations

bridge has there been extensive recent excavation and survey, and as a result this structure is now better understood. Our knowledge of the fort interior is incomplete and will remain so until further excavations using modern techniques take place. This is not to belittle the achievement of pioneers such as Clayton: without the trail they blazed, current archaeological techniques could not have developed.

CHESTERS TODAY

The remains still lie within a private estate, but in 1946 the eastern bridge abutment, and in 1954 the fort and the Wall and baths to its east, together with the museum, were placed in the guardianship of the Ministry of Works. As successor to that body, English Heritage now cares for the remains and administers the museum, together with the Trustees of the Clayton Collection. Excavation and survey took place at the eastern bridge abutment in 1982–3, and at the western in 1990–91. Otherwise there has only been occasional small-scale excavation, although much has been learnt from geophysical and other surveys. Despite the lack of recent excavation, Chesters is perhaps the most accessible and informative of all the Wall-forts. The setting alone would enchant any visitor: it has been said that 'even a Cistercian could hardly have chosen a more beautiful place'. Meanwhile the grass conceals a rich depth of buried remains, awaiting the researchers of the future.